The 'New' Atheism

The 'New' Atheism
Ten Arguments that Don't Hold Water?

Michael Poole

LION

A Lion Book
an imprint of
Lion Hudson plc
Wilkinson House, Jordan Hill Road,
Oxford OX2 8DR, England
www.lionhudson.com

ISBN 978 0 7459 5393 9

Distributed by:
UK: Marston Book Services, PO Box 269, Abingdon, Oxon,
OX14 4YN
USA: Trafalgar Square Publishing, 814 N. Franklin Street,
Chicago, IL 60610
USA Christian Market: Kregel Publications, PO Box 2607,
Grand Rapids, MI 49501

First edition 2009
10 9 8 7 6 5 4 3 2 1 0
All rights reserved

Acknowledgments
Scripture quotations taken from the *Holy Bible, New International Version*, copyright © 1973, 1978, 1984 International Bible Society. Used by permission of Zondervan and Hodder & Stoughton Limited. All rights reserved. The 'NIV' and 'New International Version' trademarks are registered in the United States Patent and Trademark Office by International Bible Society. Use of either trademark requires the permission of International Bible Society. UK trademark number 1448790.

A catalogue record for this book is available
from the British Library

Typeset in 10/13 Latin 725 BT

Printed and bound in Great Britain by J F Print Ltd, Sparkford.

Contents

Acknowledgments

I am indebted to Professor Sir Ghillean Prance, formerly Director of the Royal Botanic Gardens, Kew, and currently Scientific Director of the Eden Project, for sowing a thought in my mind which led to this book. My thanks go to Professor Prance and Professor Alister McGrath for reading and commenting upon the whole text and, for the same reason, to Andrew, my son, and especially my wife, Virginia, who has scrutinized it several times. I am also indebted to Professor Keith Ward for his helpful observations on the last chapter and to Dr Rodney Holder for comments on the multiverse section. Lastly, and importantly, I am grateful to Kate Kirkpatrick for her suggestions for improving the text at various stages of writing and to the artwork experts at Lion Hudson for embodying my cover suggestion so successfully.

Michael Poole
King's College London

About this book

This book is written for those without a lot of time for reading but who would like to see some short responses to key claims of what has, since 2006, been termed 'The New Atheism'.[1] So, what's new about it and how did it arise?

An answer to the first question will have to wait until the end of this book, but an answer to the second one was suggested by John Gray, formerly Professor of European Thought at the London School of Economics and Political Science. Having rejected both humanism and religion, he comments on the 'sudden explosion in the literature of proselytising atheism',[2] referring to Richard Dawkins' *The God Delusion*, Christopher Hitchens' *God Is Not Great*, the writings of Daniel Dennett and others. Gray argues that 'The urgency with which they produce their anti-religious polemics suggests that... the tide of secularisation has turned' and that 'the result is the appearance of an evangelical type of atheism not seen since Victorian times'.[3] Readers must judge this provocative conclusion for themselves.

This short book is mainly concerned with the writings and broadcastings of Professor Dawkins, currently the most prolific advocate of atheism. But it also examines some of the claims of the other two authors named above. I shall do my best to be fair in my criticisms of the writings of these three authors and I undertake that, if I have misrepresented their views, I will try to rectify this in any subsequent editions. Page numbers of quotations from Dawkins' and Visiting Professor Hitchens' above titles, and from Professor Daniel Dennett's *Breaking the Spell*, follow the citations, thus:[26] and[R] from Dawkins' *Root of all Evil?* TV programmes.

Since I started writing this book, quite a number of volumes on the New Atheism have appeared, but with the exception of Professor Antony Flew's *There Is a God*,[4] I took the decision not to read them before I had written what I wanted to say. However, I still owe a huge debt to that 'invisible college' of colleagues who, for decades, have stimulated my own thinking.

About the subtitle: 'Ten arguments that don't hold water?'

In an earlier philosophical work, Flew cautioned that it would not

> … do to recognize that of a whole series of arguments each individually is defective, but then to urge that nevertheless in sum they comprise an impressive case… We have here to insist upon a sometimes tricky distinction: between, on the one hand, the valid principle of the accumulation of evidence, where every item has at least some weight in its own right; and, on the other hand, the Ten-leaky-buckets-Tactic, applied to arguments none of which hold water at all.[5]

I am not suggesting that such a tactic has been deliberately employed, but rather questioning whether any of the ten points examined holds water and contribute to an overarching argument for atheism. I have interpreted Flew's caution more broadly than applying it to **A**rguments alone, to include cases where only **A**ssertions (claims to truth) seem involved without supporting arguments. At the start of each chapter I have indicated the points with which I disagree, labelling them A1–A10, to allow readers to decide for themselves whether 'A' for Argument or 'A' for Assertion turns out to be more appropriate. To constitute rational arguments, good reasons are needed, backed up by evidence for any assertions made.

In *The God Delusion*, Richard Dawkins says that, unless he indicates otherwise, he will 'have Christianity mostly in mind' as 'the version with which I happen to be most familiar'.[37] I shall follow his example and, when referring to God, I shall have the Judaeo-Christian concept of God in mind, although much of what I say will apply more widely. On matters of science, I hold the views of mainstream cosmology and biology.

Michael Poole
King's College London

Un-natural selection or 'Down with sex!'

A1 Religion is evil because many bad deeds have been done by religious people.

In a two-part television documentary entitled *Root of All Evil?*[1] Richard Dawkins selected many examples of odd, quirky or evil deeds associated with various religions in order to support his overarching thesis that 'Religion is… bad for our children and it's bad for you.'[R] To be fair, he later wrote that he disliked the title since no single thing, religion or otherwise is the root of everything. The programmes were criticized on the grounds that bad things being done in the name of religion doesn't mean that all religion is bad. If he had taken different examples, such as the evangelical William Wilberforce and the abolition of slavery, the starting and foundation of schools and hospitals, or recent testimonies of religious believers forgiving appalling deeds against them and their families, one would have seen a different – and more balanced – view of religion.

In a radio interview Richard Dawkins fairly admitted, 'I do think that's a good point and in a way that's a shortcoming of television that it's almost forced to do that.'[2] That may be, but by September of that year, his 400-page book *The God Delusion* was published, including many more negative examples.

Drawing the battle lines?

Dawkins made his purpose in publishing the book transparent, intending that 'religious readers who open it will be atheists when they put it down.'[5] Christopher Hitchens' blunt message is along the same lines: 'Religion poisons everything'; 'Religion kills.' Perhaps he should have qualified the word 'everything', in the same way that Dawkins qualified the word 'all' in the television title. It only needs *one* good deed to falsify 'all' and 'everything'! Hitchens adds, '… the mildest criticism of religion is also the most radical and the most devastating one. Religion is man-made.'[10] This assertion is paralleled by Daniel Dennett, whose book *Breaking the Spell* starts from the assumption contained in his subtitle: *Religion as a natural phenomenon*. As with Dawkins, a delusion is envisaged, a spell to be broken, since it is assumed from the start that there is no transcendent Being, only natural factors. Actually, Dennett's 'spell' turns out to be not one but two. Of the first he says, 'The spell that I say must be broken is the taboo against a forthright, scientific, no-holds-barred investigation of religion as one natural phenomenon among many.' The second 'spell' is 'religion itself'.[18] It seems surprising that the first should be counted as a spell that needs breaking. Psychologists and sociologists of religion, themselves having religious beliefs or none, have long engaged in the scientific analysis of religious behaviour as individual and group phenomena. Applying the blanket term 'scientific' to such investigations merits a word of caution, for although the types of psychological and sociological investigation I refer to are scientific ones, the Science Curriculum of one country points out that 'there are some questions that... science cannot address'.[3]

On truth

The truth, or otherwise, of the existence of God is one of these questions, a point considered further in Chapter 7. Investigators may choose to disregard the truth or falsity of religious beliefs while examining the *function* religious beliefs fulfil in the life of an individual or the structure of a society. But it must not be overlooked that the truth or falsity of the beliefs themselves is itself a valid and important study, even if it is not the immediate concern of the particular investigator. I wonder whether Dennett seems to be doing this by taking it for granted from the outset that religious beliefs about God must be false and can only have 'natural' origins, upon which he speculates.

The investigation of the functions served by religion – *functionalism* – is not, in principle, a threat to the truth-claims of religion. It is a partial, but valuable, study of one aspect of the behaviour of individual and collective humankind. Given Dennett's beliefs, he suggests

The three favourite purposes or *raisons d'être* for religion are

- **to *comfort* us in our suffering and allay our fear of death**

- **to *explain* things we can't otherwise explain**

- **to encourage group *cooperation* in the face of trials and enemies.[102f.]**

Religion serves these three functions, and why not? They say nothing about the truth or falsity of the beliefs themselves. Something that comforts us in suffering can also be true, for which we should be thankful; explanations outside the competence of science can also be true. Science cannot answer the question 'Why is there something rather than nothing?' but if God exists, it would be perfectly true and rational to say that God's activity 'explains' it, something addressed in Chapter 6.

Anyway, whether there are 'delusions', 'poison' or 'spells', the claims of these books is clear: down with religion! But all religion? All aspects of all religions? How do these writers go about their chosen task? The first two authors have collected large quantities of reports of ugly or evil things that have been associated with religion in some way. Indeed, Hitchens says, 'I have been writing this book all my life,'[285] and the quantity of bizarre stories he has amassed is large. Dennett also contributes a share but fairly comments that 'The daily actions of religious people have accomplished uncounted good deeds throughout history, alleviating suffering, feeding the hungry, caring for the sick.'[253] But neither Hitchens nor Dawkins appears to have supplied a balancing list of good acts prompted by religious beliefs.

This strategy of trawling the human race for evil deeds associated with religion results in a bad argument for dismissing religion as evil. A similar point can be made about atheists – one need only look to the mass murders of Russian communism under Stalin, Cambodian communism (Khmer Rouge) under Pol Pot, and Nazism under Hitler – but that does not mean (and it would not be fair to claim) that all atheists are genocidal or amoral.

Sex

A different example may highlight why such argumentation is bad. Suppose someone collects all the bad stories associated with sex, produces page after page of stories about broken promises, rape, adultery, promiscuity, paedophilia, lust, bestiality and pornography, and concludes that sex is bad for you and sex poisons everything. What might a happily married husband and wife think? Both religion and sex involve powerful feelings, and, where these are abused, the results can be outstandingly vile. But, equally well, they can be outstandingly good.

So I agree with Dawkins' and Hitchens' revulsions over the horrors of 'Harmful religion'. I am not defending such things; I agree with much of what they say. Neither am I giving blanket approval to every practice of all religions. Each must 'stand before the bar' for itself. People need to assess where truth lies.

Need for discernment

'Harmful religion' has much to repent of, including such Christian corruptions as the Crusades. In this example, a key question is: if something claims to be Christian, does it meet the criteria of its founder? Forgiveness is a key factor in Christianity, though not exclusively so. Furthermore, Jesus is reported as saying

> My kingdom is not of this world. If it were, my servants would fight to prevent my arrest by the Jews. But now my kingdom is from another place (John 18:36).

> By their fruit you will recognize them. Do people pick grapes from thornbushes, or figs from thistles? Likewise every good tree bears good fruit, but a bad tree bears bad fruit (Matthew 7:16–17).

In short, he is saying: if people don't do (or try to do, since we are all fallible) what I teach, don't believe them if they claim to have faith in me and to be one of my followers.

As to what 'faith' is, that is the subject of the next chapter.

'Faith is believing what you know ain't so'

A2 'Faith is irrational'[R] and 'demands a positive suspension of critical faculties.'[R]

A well-known radio interviewer provocatively said that 'science is based on evidence… and religion is, by definition, a matter of faith', something echoed in the title of this chapter by Mark Twain's famous 'schoolboy' quote. Views like this are all too common as can be seen from the following quotations: 'Religion is about turning untested belief into unshakeable trust'; 'Religious faith discourages independent thought'; 'The process of non-thinking called faith'; 'If we can retain our faith against the evidence, in the teeth of reality, the more virtuous we are.'[R] Hitchens comments:

> If one must have faith in order to believe something, or believe *in* something, then the likelihood of that something having any truth or value is considerably diminished. The harder work of inquiry, proof, and demonstration is infinitely more rewarding… [71]

... let the advocates and partisans of religion rely on faith alone, and let them be brave enough to admit that this is what they are doing.[122]

In Professor Dennett's view, people 'believe in belief', while, for Professor Grayling, 'Faith is a commitment to belief contrary to evidence and reason.'[1]

So, then, are the many religious academics involved in the sciences, some Fellows of the Royal Society, some knighted, using Dakwins' words, 'dyed-in-the-wool faith-heads', 'immune to argument', suffering from 'childhood indoctrination', not 'open-minded', 'whose native intelligence', by contrast with 'free spirits', has not been 'strong enough to break free of the vice of religion'?[5f.]

In a couple of words, it is being claimed that faith is *unevidenced belief*. But we already have a word in the English language that precisely encapsulates those qualities, and that is 'credulity'. So why not use it, rather than confusing it with 'faith'?

It is puzzling to see where this cluster of idiosyncratic 'definitions', these caricatures of faith, come from. How many religious believers would recognize *any* of them as remotely describing their own position? Are we being misled by what philosophers call '*stipulative* definitions', in the hope that, if they are uttered often enough, we will believe them?

Faith as 'trust'
The above views of faith do not reflect how the word is generally used in everyday life. In common parlance, we might express our faith in a surgeon,

a close friend's reliability, a particular medicine, a bungee rope and the integrity of a husband/wife.

Of course, faith *can* turn out to be misplaced, even though sincerely held. Sincerity, though praiseworthy, is not enough. Someone might take from their garden shed a bottle of what they sincerely believed was water, to extinguish the glowing charcoal of a spent barbecue. But their sincerity would not help if the colourless liquid in the bottle was petrol for the lawnmower. Or again, until recently most people would have sincerely believed that faith in a bank's secure keeping of their savings was beyond question.

So, what about Dennett's phrase about having 'faith in faith'? Could one then have faith in faith in faith? Somehow these phrases sound linguistically odd. That is because 'faith' is a word that cannot stand alone. Faith has to be *in* something or somebody, and the reliability or otherwise of the object of faith is of key importance.

A group of Scouts constructed a rope bridge across a river. Pleased with what they had done, they had enough faith in their efforts to believe they could safely cross the river. and they were not disappointed. But this act of faith drew upon earlier experience, perhaps of failures, knowing about the required thickness of the ropes and the best positioning of the guy-ropes. Similarly, faith in entrusting our lives to an anaesthetist draws on some understanding of medical practice and the testimonies of those who have come safely through operations under general anaesthetics.

So, why redefine 'faith' for the purpose of discrediting it in religion and trying to make the new definition – again using philosophical language – a *persuasive* definition? A synonym for 'faith' is 'trust' – trust in the safety of a shaky rope bridge or trust in a person, who might be a doctor, a spouse or a garage mechanic. So what sort of sense would it make to speak of 'trust in trust' or even 'trust in trust in trust'?

An unexpected encounter

A lady dropped her purse without noticing and I retrieved it and handed it back to her. The lady turned out to be Winifred Blondin, who lived to the ripe old age of 106. Many stories are told of her grandfather's amazing exploits as a tightrope walker. On 30 June 1859,[2] he crossed the gorge of Niagara Falls on a tightrope. Other times he pushed a wheelbarrow across and even cycled over. Crowds were enthusiastic and he is said to have asked a bystander if he thought he, Blondin, could push a man across in the wheelbarrow. 'Yes,' said the bystander confidently. Blondin replied, 'Jump in!' – and you couldn't see the man for dust! The story highlights 'faith' as more than just 'believing that'; it is 'belief + action', 'trusting in' – something, unsurprisingly, the bystander did not feel able to do.

It is not appropriate to treat faith as a blind leap in the dark. That could be fatal. People have been known to do that in the night, trapped at the top of a burning building. But if someone in that predicament, blinded by smoke, heard the sound of a fire engine's siren and a loudspeaker announcing the fire brigade's presence with a safety net, then an act of faith, of trust in what was already believable from prior evidence, would be rational. In a word, to avoid foolhardy *credulity*, there needs to be rationality based on evidence.

Rationality

Rationality is the belief, the act of faith, that our thought processes are basically reliable. This belief underpins every human activity – even debating the belief in rationality! It is a presupposition which, if untrue, would make our speaking just noises and our writing mere squiggles.

The same points apply to atheists, and it is not clear how Dawkins can justifiably assert that 'Atheists do not have faith...'[51], especially having stated earlier that 'An atheist in this sense of philosophical naturalist is somebody who believes [that is, has faith that] there is nothing beyond the natural, physical world...'[14] Neither does it fit with Dawkins' appeal, in the first of his Christmas lectures, to 'Put your faith in the scientific method. There's nothing wrong with having faith... there's nothing wrong with having faith in a proper scientific prediction.'

Like it or not, 'faith' is a word used by religious and non-religious people. So are there other words used to denigrate religion that can turn round and bite their owners?

People who live in glass houses... ?

A3 Religious beliefs are memes, mind viruses, self-delusion, placebos, wishful thinking and indoctrination.

Most of us fall into the trap of thinking that our own generalizations apply to everyone except ourselves. If someone says, 'Nobody tells the truth these days', would you believe them? Philosophers have a polite way of saying 'You too!' They say it in Latin: 'Tu quoque!' If a postmodernist asserts that 'There is no such thing as absolute truth', what are the consequences for postmodernism of agreeing/disagreeing with that statement? It is easy to forget this principle of reflexivity, this *double-edged sword that cuts both ways.*

Memes and mind viruses

Dawkins suggested in *The Selfish Gene* that 'a new kind of replicator has recently emerged on this very planet... a unit of cultural transmission or a unit of *imitation*'. Rejecting the label of 'mimeme', with its suggestion of 'mimic', in favour of a single-syllable word analogous to *gene,* he arrived at 'meme'.[1] There have been divided views about the value or otherwise of coining a special term to refer to the familiar idea of passing on cultural practices, as well as considerable concern about the propriety of applying the word 'selfish' to genes.

Memes in themselves can be neutral in their connotation, as with 'names, ideas, catch-phrases, clothes fashions'.[2] Dawkins also employs negatively slanted memes such as 'Faith' – 'It means blind trust'[3] – and 'the god meme'.[4] Dennett, although favouring the concept of 'memes', is willing to acknowledge that there can be 'atheist memes'. So, there seems to be no religious or atheistic mileage in the concept until you choose the name of the meme, only a debate about whether the concept of meme is redundant.

'Mind virus', as a metaphor for religious beliefs, captures the implication of unpleasantness, in order to persuade others that religion is evil, as well as depicting the idea of replication by passing from person to person. The latter property, however, is metaphorically benign, since happiness can replicate, passing from person to person.

A word of caution about using the term 'mind viruses' comes from Dennett:

Although this jarring claim needs to be considered as a major possibility, we should not forget that the vast majority of memes, like the vast majority of bacterial and viral symbionts that inhabit our bodies, are neutral or even helpful (from the perspective of host fitness).[184]

Nevertheless Dawkins proceeds with his metaphor and claims that 'Like computer viruses, successful mind viruses will tend to be hard for their victims to detect. If you are the victim of one, the chances are that you won't know it, and may even vigorously deny it.'[5]

Self-delusion

But if belief in a God is a 'mind virus' that we may not know we have, then the double-edged sword that cuts both ways dictates that belief in no God is also a 'mind virus' that we may not know we have. This leaves the awful possibility that the atheist, too, may be living a life of total self-delusion without knowing it.

Placebos

The 'god meme… provides a superficially plausible answer to deep and troubling questions about existence… The "everlasting arms" hold out a cushion against our own inadequacies which, like a doctor's placebo, is none the less effective for being imaginary'.[6]

Dawkins uses a carefully chosen simile, loaded against religious faith being true, to raise a question (also asked by Dennett): like a placebo, 'Even if we accept that God doesn't exist… Isn't it consoling? Doesn't it motivate people to do good?'[158f.] This is an *instrumentalist* approach to religion: never mind whether it is true or not, what does it *do*? Is it *useful*? As might be anticipated, Dawkins answers 'no' to instrumentalism and recognizes truth as important. So are religious beliefs what atheists accuse them of being, namely…

Wishful thinking

This is a term usually applied to something that cannot be realized because the wish will not, or cannot, be fulfilled. According to Dawkins, belief in immortality illustrates 'the wishful thinking of religion'[188] but, by contrast, 'The atheist view is correspondingly life-affirming and life-enhancing… never being tainted with self-delusion, wishful thinking…' [361] Furthermore, Dawkins claims that 'people of a theological bent are often chronically incapable of distinguishing what is true from what they'd like to be true.'[108] But here comes the double-edged sword that cuts both ways. Change 'theological' for 'atheistic' and where does that get us in the debate?

Indoctrination

The word 'indoctrination' is a 'Boo!' word. *Indoctrination* is what 'they' do; *education* (a 'Yay!' word) is what 'we' do. If 'we' *really* dislike what 'they' are teaching, then it may be called *brainwashing*. All this is usually with little attention to philosophical niceties such as whether the charge of indoctrination refers to the *method*, *content*, *consequences* or *intentions* of the teacher and, in the case of brainwashing, disregards the absence of bright lights, sleep deprivation, humiliation, interrogation and physical pain, or fear of pain. As far as I am aware, neither

Dawkins nor Hitchens uses the latter term, but both refer to 'indoctrination'.

Dawkins is concerned about what he sees as the indoctrination of young people arising because, although unquestioning belief in what their parents and elders say carries with it an evolutionary selective advantage, it can be exploited.

But if young people really are as easily taken in as Dawkins seems to think, then there awaits another double-edged sword that cuts both ways. The persistence of *atheism* could also owe a lot to the gullibility of young people. But many children *are* taught to question and think through their beliefs; and some, after careful thought, arrive at belief in God or retain their existing belief in God.

One would hardly expect parents to teach their children the opposite to what they hold to be true! Children soon learn, through contact with other children, that not all children believe what their own parents may believe, so they start asking questions. In various of the world's education systems young people learn about other religions and 'stances for living'.

So perhaps the dangers are not as real as Dawkins seems to think. It is reasonable not to stick the labels of the parent's faith on to children who are too young to have made individual commitments. But, on the other hand, children can come into an experience of trusting in God at an early age. After all, childlike – but not childish – trust is a prerequisite, since 'anyone who will not receive the kingdom of God like a little child will never enter it' (Mark 10:15 and Luke 18:17). Francis Bacon introduced a thought-provoking parallel when he wrote in his 1620 *Novum Organum*, 'the entrance into the Kingdom of man, founded on the sciences, being not much other than the entrance into the Kingdom of Heaven, where into none may enter except as a little child'.

A couple who gave their children this opportunity, and taught them that God is interested is every aspect of their lives, went on a shopping expedition. They discovered they had left a carrier-bag of goods in one of many shops they had visited. Their nine-year-old son was concerned, so the father said, 'Why don't you pray about it?' The son, being articulate and uninhibited, did so on the spot and an interesting series of events unfolded. The family drew a blank in one shop, because a different person who was then serving said the bag was not there – although actually it was. In another shop a customer overheard the repeated enquiry about the bag and said that the bag *had* been found in the first shop when she had been there earlier. So back the family trekked and retrieved the bag. It was Sir William Temple who said, 'When I pray, coincidences happen, and when I don't, they don't.'

Tu quoque?

Dawkins' 1991 Christmas lectures 'Growing up in the Universe' can now be viewed online or purchased on DVDs through his website, The Richard Dawkins Foundation for Reason and Science. The site encourages viewers to get these recordings into schools and libraries. So, presumably, this can be taken as Dawkins' approval of what he said in 1991.

If so, it also appears to justify some of the criticisms made at the time.

The quality of Dawkins' lectures and of the BBC production was excellent, but for one thing – what appeared as the unjustified intrusion of numerous anti-religious comments throughout the series. They were not warranted by the science and conveyed the misleading picture to the youthful audience that science leads to atheism, without any indication of an alternative position. This was not best practice in education then, or now, and complaints were made following the lectures.[7] So does the republishing of these lectures at the present time unsheath the double-edged sword that cuts both ways? Is Dawkins perpetuating a practice he disapproves of in others?

Furthermore, in the recent award-winning series *The Genius of Charles Darwin,* an allied problem arises. In the first programme, Dawkins takes a group of fifteen- and sixteen-year-olds and sets out to convince them of the truth of evolution, and, as ever, argues the case well. But when a student expresses his religious beliefs, Dawkins makes an aside, but not to the class: 'I can see that a few hours in the science lab is no match for a lifetime of religious indoctrination.' In the absence of the students, he asserts that 'Darwin's theory explained how the diversity of life on the planet had evolved spontaneously, without interference from any God.' But, logically, there can be no evidence that understanding the processes of biological adaptation rules out divine action in bringing about and maintaining such processes. His audience appeared confused, both early on and at the end of the programme, about seeming to have to choose between evolution and belief in God. This is hardly surprising as it illustrates the *fallacy of the excluded middle*, presenting a choice between only two positions when others are logically possible. It is coherent to believe *both* that adaptation occurs through evolution by natural selection *and* that this process is God's creative work. At the end of the programme, there appeared to be a marked reluctance by those students who believed in God to relinquish that belief on account of the excellent presentation of evolution. If they had heard of the fallacy of the excluded middle, they might have realized they didn't have to make such a choice.

'... and may be used in evidence'?

A4 'Faith (belief without evidence) is a virtue. The more your beliefs defy the evidence, the more virtuous you are.' [199]

The existence of God is a controversial issue about which opposite views can rationally be held. Faith and reason are not opposites; neither are faith and facts (or evidence), unless credulity is in mind. Nevertheless, both these false dichotomies are repeated countlessly. The factual element is the *object* of faith. But we need to bear in mind that an act of faith, of believing, is not simply a *cognitive* matter. It also engages the *affective* domains of the emotions and the will. The present concern is, however, with cognitive factors: the *grounds*, the *evidence,* the means of *justification* for faith.

In *Root of all Evil?* Dawkins states that 'Science weighs evidence and advances. Religion is hide-bound belief for belief's sake...' and '... the whole point about faith is that even massive and constantly accumulating physical evidence cuts no ice.' But is this true?

Evidence for God?

John Montgomery, Professor Emeritus of Law and Humanities, tells how Mortimer Adler, an American educator and philosopher, approached the evidence for the existence of God in his book *How to Think about God*.[1] Adler did not consider himself a religious believer at the time of publication, but nevertheless he,

> **at the end of his careful discussion of God's existence, employs, not the traditional philosophical ideal of Cartesian absolute certainty, but the legal standards of proof by preponderance of evidence and proof beyond reasonable doubt: 'If I am able to say no more than that a preponderance of reasons favour believing that God exists, I can still say I have advanced reasonable grounds for that belief...'[2]**

In other words, the belief is rational. Proof, beyond any doubt whatever, belongs largely to formal logic and certain branches of mathematics. 'Proof' – as testing, trying out, demonstrating, as in the phrase 'the proof of the pudding is in the eating' – expresses a general and more realistic way of using the word. But what kinds of evidence are there?

- *direct* evidence, such as the witnessing of a crime;
- *indirect* evidence, such as the cloud-chamber track of an electron or a footprint at the scene of a crime;
- *cumulative* evidence, as in a court of law. Here and

elsewhere, many small pieces of evidence, none of which by themselves might be fully persuasive, may add up to a convincing case based on 'the legal standards of proof by preponderance of evidence and proof beyond reasonable doubt'. A footprint by itself may not be enough, but similar mud from the location of the footprint on a suspect's shoes may help strengthen the case.

So, how might all this be applied to belief in God? Since 'No one has ever seen God', as John's Gospel puts it (1:18), *direct* evidence is not possible. We might, however, ask whether something akin to this takes place when John records Jesus saying, 'Anyone who has seen me has seen the Father. How can you say, "Show us the Father"?' (John 14:9). But is this quite the same thing as 'seeing' the 'invisible God'?

On this central doctrine of Christian belief, the *incarnation* – the *embodying* of God – Dawkins makes the surprising generalization that 'The historical evidence that Jesus claimed any sort of divine status is minimal... there is no good historical evidence that he ever thought he was divine.'[92] In this instance, reading the four Gospels would be an appropriate rebuttal. Here are samples from each of the four Gospel writers:

- Matthew (26:63–66): 'The high priest said... "Tell us if you are the Christ, the Son of God." "Yes, it is as you say," Jesus replied.'
- Mark (2:7): 'Why does this fellow talk like that? He's blaspheming! Who can forgive sins but God alone?'
- Luke (22:70): '[The chief priests and teachers of

the law] asked, "Are you then the Son of God?" He replied, "You are right in saying I am."'
- John (10:33): '... the Jews [replied] "... you, a mere man, claim to be God."'

These testimonies illustrate the point that evidence today will have to be *indirect* – reported speech. Tests for the reliability of these authors, as well as of other historians such as Tacitus, Pliny and Josephus, draw upon the usual canons of historical evidence.

A cumulative case

So, what pieces of *cumulative* evidence, each having *some* small value, can add up to 'proof by preponderance of evidence and proof beyond reasonable doubt', while steering clear of the Ten-Leaky-Buckets-Tactic explained in the preface? There are, of course, 'standard arguments' for the existence of God, such as Aquinas' 'Five Ways', which feature in introductions to theology. These arguments are not above criticism, although that may not prevent them having *some* value in constructing a cumulative case, which may include:

1. That there is a world. There is something rather than nothing, raising questions such as 'What brought it into existence?'
2. The kind of world it is. This suggests 'an argument *to* design *from* order... and, thus, a "Designer"', as Professor Antony Flew[3] succinctly puts it in the interesting story of his recent pilgrimage from almost a lifetime of atheism to saying 'I now believe there is a God!'[4] In this

book, subtitled 'How the world's most notorious atheist changed his mind', Flew recounts that 'my discovery of the Divine has been a pilgrimage of reason and not of faith'.[5] This is because he adhered to the Socratic principle, 'We must follow the argument wherever it leads'[6] – a principle that I am sure Dawkins would endorse, albeit to a different conclusion. Among the reasons for his change, Flew cites, 'Science spotlights three dimensions of nature that point to God... that nature obeys laws... the dimensions of life, of intelligently organised and purpose-driven beings... the very existence of nature'[7] (my number 1). The Earth's suitability for life as we know it is considered in Chapter 10.

3. The existence of beauty and moral values, including appeals to innate ideas of obligation and fairness.

4. Revelation of things that we could not otherwise know, of which Flew says, 'I have taken issue with many of the claims of divine revelation or intervention. My current position, however, is more open to at least certain of these claims.'[8]

5. The evidential value of religious experience, including answered prayer. This, to the believer, is perhaps the most important. On one occasion Darwin wrote:

At the present day the most usual argument for the existence of an intelligent God is drawn from the deep inward conviction and feelings which are experienced by most persons.[9]

Personal experience directs talk about God

away from the realm of speculation about whether the 'transcendent, conscious agency' of the philosophers exists, to considering the realm of personal experience. But this is in the private domain, which is largely inaccessible to others unless the person chooses to tell. The nearest glimpse the outsider may have might be the personal testimony of the believer, along with a changed character and lifestyle. Such factors belong to the public domain and can be scrutinized by a third party.

6. Historical evidence, drawing on both secular and religious sources. It is simplistic to dismiss the latter because 'they have an axe to grind'. They need to be accorded the same careful scrutiny – and value – as the secular ones, which may also have an axe to grind. Dennett begins his section 'Does God Exist?' by considering

... the arguments from presumed historical documentation, such as this: according to the Bible, which is the literal truth, God exists, has always existed, and created the universe in seven days a few thousand years ago. The historical arguments are apparently satisfying to those who accept them, but they simply cannot be introduced into a serious investigation, since they are manifestly question-begging.[240]

But why should this be so? As a general point about interpretation, the author of the third Gospel, Luke, is widely regarded by historians as paying great attention to historical detail. So, if he is truthful about matters that *can* be checked, does this not increase the likelihood of his integrity in matters which, currently,

cannot? On the specific point of the interpretation
of the Genesis account of creation, which Luke does
not address, Augustine (AD 354–430), like Origen (c.
AD 185–254) before him, rejected the interpretation
cited by Dennett, that God 'created the universe in
seven [*sic*] days' (of 'twenty-four hours'). Augustine
wrote, none too politely,

> **Usually, even a non-Christian knows something about
> the earth, the heavens, and the other elements of this
> world... If they find a Christian mistaken in a field which
> they themselves know well and hear him maintaining
> his foolish opinions about our books, how are they
> going to believe those books in matters concerning the
> resurrection of the dead, the hope of eternal life, and the
> kingdom of heaven...?[10]**

Augustine is making a similar point, but in reverse,
to the one I have just made, namely that if people
read 'foolish opinions' about the Earth and heavens
into Genesis, others will be less inclined to believe
the Bible on matters less familiar to them, such as
those listed in his last two lines. Augustine, and
Origen realized that the 'days' were unlikely to mean
'twenty-four hours' since the sun and stars – the only
ways of measuring days, mornings and evenings –
were not 'created' until day four!

Dennett's comment and Augustine's highlight
the point that due care must be taken of the literary
genre of the particular writings under review. To treat
literary devices such as elevated prose, metaphors,
parables and allegories literally can make nonsense
of their meanings.

Evidence against God?

The problem of reconciling pain and suffering with a loving God (theodicy) has often been cited as counter-evidence for God. This difficulty is referred to again in Chapter 9. In the mid-twentieth century there was a lively philosophical debate about whether belief in the existence of God could be falsified. Flew, then writing from his earlier position of atheism, posed the question: 'What would have to occur or to have occurred to constitute for you a disproof of the love of, or of the existence of God?'[11] This much-debated request for a *falsification criterion*, as it was called, actually has a straightforward answer to the claim to truth of one religion, Christianity, as being the resurrection of its founder. The apostle Paul wrote in his first letter to the church at Corinth that '... if Christ has not been raised, your faith is futile' (1 Corinthians 15:17). If there is no resurrection, Christianity crumbles. Paul records what would have been a convincing number of witnesses to persuade others around at the time (1 Corinthians 15:5–8), and his writings can be examined as part of the indirect evidence available to those alive today.

Hitchens comments that 'according to the New Testament, the thing [raising from the dead] could be done in an almost commonplace way. Jesus managed it twice in other people's cases, by raising both Lazarus and the daughter of Jairus...'[142] and that 'This supposed frequency of resurrection can only undermine the uniqueness of the one by which mankind purchased forgiveness of sins.' [143] What is missing from his glance at those three episodes is that Lazarus and the daughter of Jairus died again. Hitchens also says, 'Again we might call upon the trusty Ockham, who warned us not to multiply unnecessary contingencies. Thus let me give one ancient and one modern example: the first being bodily resurrection...' [141] But it is not clear how Ockham's razor, introduced in Chapter 6, can be applied to dismiss Jesus' resurrection. As the *falsification criterion* of Christianity, it can hardly class among 'unnecessary contingencies'.

Dawkins, however, in his rightful insistence on evidence, does not appear to tackle the evidential claim of the resurrection. But surely this is *the* factor to concentrate on if he particularly wants to discredit Christianity. It goes straight to the jugular. Demolish this claim and the falsification is complete, without further argument. As a claimed unique event, it is a historical question. The way matter normally behaves, enshrined in scientific laws, is not going to help here. Other approaches are needed. If Jesus was simply a man, his claim 'I have authority to lay it [my life] down and authority to take it up again' (John 10:18) is surely outrageous.

But if he is, as Christians believe, God incarnate, the agent of creating and upholding the universe,[12] then against the backdrop of creating a hundred thousand million galaxies, each containing a hundred thousand million stars, a resurrection might not seem so difficult!

Many have attempted to disprove the resurrection story but, so far, without notable success. So here appears to be a fruitful avenue for continuing atheist research. It is not without possible perils, however. A journalist, writing under the *nom de plume* of Frank

Morison, intended to write a book to support his earlier belief that Jesus' 'history rested upon very insecure foundations'. *Who Moved the Stone?*[13] – now in its eighteenth printing – reads rather like a detective story. It describes how the author 'set out to write one kind of book and found himself compelled by the sheer force of circumstances to write quite another'.[14]

Simon Greenleaf, Professor of Law at Harvard University, who is credited with producing 'the greatest single authority on evidence in the entire literature of legal procedure', also carried out an investigation into the reliability of the Gospel writers and wrote:

Either the men of Galilee were men of superlative wisdom, and extensive knowledge and experience, and of deeper skill in the arts of deception than any and all others, before or after them, or they have truly stated the astonishing things which they saw and heard.[15]

Flew, writing from his new position, remarks, 'Today, I would say the claim concerning the resurrection is more impressive than any by the religious competition.'[16] His comment introduces the subject of the next chapter: the biblical records.

5

Ancient.doc

A5 '… Dan Brown's novel **The Da Vinci Code**… *is indeed fabricated from start to finish: invented, made-up fiction. In that respect, it is exactly like the gospels.'*[97]

[Maimonides, a great Jewish scholar] 'fell into the same error as do the Christians, in assuming that the four Gospels were in any sense a historical record'.[Hitchens 111]

In the last chapter, one of the sources of cumulative evidence cited was the biblical records, and since both Dawkins and Hitchens have made numerous comments about these, a little more needs to be said about them.

Eleven words say a lot

A boy once said to his religious education teacher, 'My Dad says the Bible is a load of old rubbish.' The teacher drew a deep breath and thought, 'Where do you start?' The book was written by about forty different authors over some fifteen hundred years, and vast amounts of time and scholarly expertise have been expended upon it. But in eleven words the boy dismissed all this and more.

Might the teacher's reaction have been similar on reading some of Dawkins' and Hitchens' generalizations? After sensibly dismissing 'crude miracle stories' like the ones in the apocryphal Gospel of Thomas, Dawkins claims,

> there is no more and no less reason to believe the four canonical gospels. All have the status of legends, as factually dubious as the stories of King Arthur and his Knights of the Round Table.[96]

> Although Jesus probably existed, reputable biblical scholars [Dawkins cites none here] do not in general regard the New Testament (and obviously not the Old Testament) as a reliable record of what actually happened in history, and I shall not consider the Bible further as evidence for any kind of deity.[97]

Hitchens makes his view clear in the words of the journalist H. L. Menken, saying,

> I shall again defer to a finer writer than myself and quote what H. L. Menken irrefutably [sic] says... 'The simple fact is that the New Testament, as we know it, is a helter-skelter accumulation of more or less discordant documents, some of them probably of respectable origin but others palpably apocryphal, and that most of them, the good along with the bad, show unmistakable signs of having been tampered with.'[110]

Few people would dispute the stature of H. L. Menken as a journalist but others might consider it more appropriate to have quoted an authority on the New Testament.

Hitchens says of the four Gospels, 'Their multiple authors – none of whom published anything until many decades after the Crucifixion – cannot agree on anything of importance.'[111] This last claim is a surprising one. All agree on the life, miraculous powers, crucifixion and resurrection of Jesus for a start!

Apart from these generalizations, for reasons of space I am only going to mention a few specific points. Hitchens goes on to list some matters he sees as problems concerning the place of Jesus' birth, which Dawkins also refers to. Hitchens says,

> ... the jumbled 'Old' Testament prophecies indicate that the Messiah will be born in the city of David, which seems indeed to have been Bethlehem. However, Jesus's parents were apparently from Nazareth and if they had a child he was most probably delivered in that town.[114]

That word 'probably' again! The 'jumbled "Old" Testament prophecies' are in fact a single verse from the prophet Micah (5:2), mentioned by Dawkins, which refers to Bethlehem. Dawkins comments, 'In the light of this prophecy, John's Gospel specifically remarks that his followers were surprised that he was *not* born in Bethlehem.'[93] But John's Gospel does not say Jesus' 'followers'. What John's Gospel *does* say is:

> On hearing his words, some of the people [Greek *ochlos*, crowd] said, 'Surely this man is the Prophet.' Others

said, 'He is the Christ.' Still others asked, 'How can the
Christ come from Galilee? Does not the Scripture say
that the Christ will come from David's family and from
Bethlehem, the town where David lived?' Thus the people
[*ochlos*] were divided because of Jesus (John 7:40–43).

There was no particular reason why that crowd
should know that a journey to Bethlehem had been
made some thirty years earlier.

Again, Hitchens and Dawkins question the accounts
of the journey to Bethlehem and the flight into Egypt.
Since a key theme of this book is the interplay between
religion and science, it is appropriate to reflect on
the contributions that science can make to resolving
some disputes of this kind. A scholarly treatment of
these events was published in the *Quarterly Journal
of the Royal Astronomical Society* under the title of 'The
Star of Bethlehem – a Comet in 5 BC – and the Date
of the Birth of Christ'.[1] In this article the different
details recorded by Matthew and Luke are put
together, suggesting a plausible sequence of events.
I am not saying that either this article or 'Dating the
Crucifixion' (referred to below) is the last word on
these topics; simply that these events cannot just be
written off when scholarly, peer-reviewed journals
of national repute consider them worth publishing.
Science also provides interesting insights into the
crossings of the Red Sea and the River Jordan, the
plagues in Egypt and the destruction of Sodom and
Gomorrah.

A general point about understanding and
interpreting historical records of two thousand years
ago is that questions often arise that require patient

study and scholarship; there are no quick fixes. After all, it was not so long ago, before the discovery of the 'Pilate Stone' in Capernaum, that sceptics doubted the existence of Pontius Pilate.

Finally, on a major matter, whereas Dawkins seems to fluctuate between 'Jesus probably existed'[97] and '... Jesus, if he existed (or whoever wrote his script if he didn't)'[250], Hitchens criticizes C. S. Lewis because he 'assumes on no firm evidence whatever that Jesus actually *was* a "character in history"'[119] In similar vein, he says, 'The best argument I know for the highly questionable existence of Jesus is this. His illiterate living disciples left us no record and in any event could not have been "Christians" since they were never to read those later books in which Christians must affirm belief ...'[114] Likewise, Dawkins says, 'Nobody knows who the four evangelists were, but they almost certainly never met Jesus personally.'[96] This 'almost certainly' assertion is especially puzzling when, for instance, there appears to be good evidence that the fourth Gospel was the work of the apostle John, who was closely involved with Jesus.[2] The Gospels *are* key records. The statement 'could not have been "Christians"' prompts a reminder that 'The disciples were called Christians first at Antioch' (Acts 11:26), something comparable to the nickname 'Methodists' given to the Wesleys and their supporters.

These and other speculations, with their 'probably' and 'almost certainly', raise questions as to how the authors could possibly know, without claiming some privileged insights that the rest of us do not have. Following some of these dismissive comments about the historicity of Jesus, it is worth pointing out that religion and science have once again shared, through historical documents and ancient astronomical records, in offering a precise date of 3 April AD 33 for the crucifixion of this 'highly questionable' figure. 'Dating the Crucifixion'[3] was published in the prestigious journal *Nature*.

The ancient.doc rule

John Montgomery (p.31), in his paper 'A Lawyer's Defence of Christianity', comments that

> In a court of law, admissible evidence is considered truthful unless impeached or otherwise rendered doubtful. This is in accord with ordinary life, where only the paranoiac goes about with the bias that everyone is lying.[4]

Montgomery mentions how Professor Simon Greenleaf, referred to in Chapter 4,

> ... applied to these [New Testament] records the "ancient documents" rule: ancient documents will be received as competent evidence if they are "fair on their face" (i.e. offer no internal evidence of tampering) and have been maintained in "reasonable custody"... He concluded that the competence of the New Testament documents would be established in any court of law.[5]

Some concluding observations

F. F. Bruce, sometime Rylands Professor of Biblical Criticism and Exegesis in the University of Manchester, commented:

> ... if the New Testament were a collection of secular writings, their authenticity would generally be regarded as beyond all doubt. It is a curious fact that historians have often been much readier to trust the New Testament records than have many theologians. Somehow or other, there are people who regard a 'sacred book' as *ipso facto* under suspicion, and demand much more corroborative evidence for such a work than they would for an ordinary secular or pagan writing. From the viewpoint of the historian, the same standards must be applied to both.[6]

He was referring to those who say we should treat the Bible like any other book, but who themselves treat the Bible like no other book. They adopt a 'hermeneutics of suspicion' by approaching every text with scepticism.

Eric Ives, Emeritus Professor of History, University of Birmingham, observed:

> One point about the New Testament texts which must impress the historian is that they are very extensive compared with other writings of the period. All we know of Tacitus' *Annals and Histories* is preserved in two manuscripts; his minor works survive in a single copy... the earliest Tacitus dates from the ninth century AD, and so too does Caesar's *Gallic War*...
>
> By contrast, New Testament manuscripts are plentiful, early and varied.[7]

Bruce pointed out, 'There are in existence about 5,000 Greek manuscripts of the New Testament in whole or in part.'[8] Ives concludes:

> ... the writings of the early Fathers also preserve the

traditions and memories of the Christians who lived between fifty and a hundred years after the death of Christ… the conclusion seems inescapable: there is overwhelming evidence that the New Testament documents are authentic sources for the life of Jesus Christ and the faith of his immediate disciples.[9]

Whereas there are differences of opinion among scholars, the above views of professionals in the field make the comments of Dawkins and Hitchens on biblical interpretation seem inappropriately dismissive.

Explaining explaining

6

A6 *'Historically, religion aspired to
explain our own existence and the nature
of the universe ... In this role it is now
completely superseded by science...'* [347]

*'Religion has run out of justifications.
Thanks to the telescope and the
microscope, it no longer offers
an explanation of anything
important.'* [Hitchens 28]

*'Religion can only provide facile,
ultimately unsatisfying answers. Science is
constantly seeking real explanations...'* [R]

The last two chapters have focused on evidence in
general – direct, indirect and cumulative – and types of
evidence in particular, concluding with historical and
scientific evidence for people and events in the past.
'Evidence' is something *evident* that gives grounds for
believing something else. Different types of evidence

provide the basis for *different types of explanation* – the subject of this chapter.

Making light of it?

'Why is the kitchen light on?' asks a father of his scientifically minded son.

Something *evident* – the fluorescent light being on – gives grounds for believing other things: (1) electricity passing through a tube and (2) the action of an *agent*, the son. So, the son might have replied, 'Because an electric current flowing through a gas at low pressure transfers energy to the ionized gases. This raises their atoms into higher energy orbits. When they fall back down from these, they re-emit the energy in the form of radiation. This in its turn excites the phosphor coating on the inside of the tube, causing it to emit light.'

Or (however unlikely), 'Because I wanted to be able to see to do the washing-up when I'd finished watching TV.'

A third explanation, the one the father wanted, and probably clear from his tone of voice, was an answer to 'Why, with electricity costs soaring, do you keep leaving lights on all over the house when you aren't there?'

Explaining something, as the name suggests, is making it *plain*, and usually, as the story indicates, there can be different *types* of explanation, rather than just one, *the* explanation. In the example given, the first is a *scientific* explanation, obviously not required, while the second and third are explanations about the purposes and ethical responsibilities of an *agent*, the son.

Simple or complicated explanations?

In the fourteenth century, a philosopher/theologian who came to be known as William of Ockham (or Occam) suggested that simple explanations were better than complicated ones. He expressed this in the phrase 'It is vain to do with more what can be done with fewer.' Although this is sometimes rephrased as 'Don't multiply entities beyond necessity', Ockham himself does not appear to have used this form of words. His suggestion is referred to as Ockham's *razor* because it cuts away what is superfluous. It is a principle of economy in explanations, widely followed in science and elsewhere.

Ockham's razor has been claimed to teach that scientific explanations of the universe, and life itself, render religious explanations redundant. But is this so? Hitchens refers to attempts to reconcile suffering and free will with a good God (theodicy) in

> ... the ancient enquiry of Epicurus "Is he [God] willing to prevent evil but not able? Then is he impotent. Is he able but not willing? Then is he malevolent. Is he both able and willing? Whence then is evil?"

and answers, 'Atheism cuts through this non-quandary like the razor of Ockham.'[268] No God, no quandary! Hitchens believes that Ockham's principle eliminates 'supernatural' explanations, including miracles:

> Those who desire to certify miracles may wish to say that such recoveries [from ill health] have no 'natural' explanation. But this does not at all mean that there is

therefore a 'supernatural' one... Once again the razor of Ockham is clean and decisive. When two explanations are offered, one must discard the one that explains the least, or explains nothing at all, or raises more questions than it answers.[147f.]

Does this mean *any* two explanations? Suppose a patient is cured of a disease. *An* explanation – not *the* (only) explanation – of why the patient recovered could be 'because the antibiotics killed the bacteria'. But another explanation is 'because the doctor correctly diagnosed the disease and administered antibiotics'. The two distinct *types* of explanations are logically *compatible*. More generally, there is no question of having to choose between (1) the *scientific processes* involved and (2) the action of an *agent* – in this case the doctor, but the point still applies if the agent is God.

A believer in God

William of Ockham was a theologian and a philosopher. He believed in God and certainly wasn't denying God's existence because other types of explanations are applicable. In fact, he thought that there were some things that could *only* be known by divine revelation. Although others might misapply his principle of simplicity to try to eliminate everything religious, this was not what William of Ockham was saying. His choice involved the simplest explanation of the *same kind*. It seems that Hitchens actually highlights this point by quoting Ockham as saying 'It is difficult or impossible... to prove against the philosophers that there cannot be an infinite regress in causes of the same kind.'[71]

Hitchens uses this quotation in order to introduce his claim, parallel to Dawkins' own, that 'the possibility of a designer or creator only raises the unanswerable question of who designed the designer or created the creator'.[71] The claim of an infinite regress will be examined in Chapter 10. The only relevant words for the moment are 'causes of *the same kind*' because they highlight a failure to recognize this condition as central to muddles about Ockham's razor. Causes of *different* kinds – the act of a doctor/the workings of an antibiotic in healing a patient – involve logically distinct, but compatible, *types* of explanation, all having a right to be there, even if not all are needed at once. So a key question raised by Ockham's principle is: which explanations are *needed* and which are not?

Compatible explanations

A common mistake is to regard explanations of *processes* as alternatives to explanations about the *acts* of agents, human or divine, rather than as compatible accounts. In connection with science-and-religion issues, this tendency sometimes manifests itself not simply as contentment with one type of explanation but in denying the need, the validity, or both, of other types of explanation. 'People used to think, "In the beginning God created the heavens and the Earth", but now scientists tell us, "In the beginning there was a Big Bang".' Comments like these trip easily off the tongue, and the conversation may move on before there is time to say, 'Hey, wait a minute; couldn't it be both? Surely, saying "God made it" is logically compatible with saying *how* it came about, isn't it? One is an explanation of the action of an *agent* (God); the other is a different *type* of explanation about the processes involved.' So, referring to what Hitchens sees as a historical dilemma –

It is not quite possible to locate the exact moment when men of learning stopped spinning the coin as between a creator and a long complex process...[66]

– it turns out that no coin tossing is needed, or justified. Both can be true. It is frequently the case that there is more than one type of explanation for something – here 'a creator' and 'a long complex process' – even though we might not be interested in more than one type at a time. Although references to God used to occur in early scientific works, such as Newton's famous *Principia Mathematica*, that practice has largely disappeared. This is because you do not *need* to bring in talk about God to do science – any more than you need to bring in talk about Rudolf Diesel to describe how a compression-ignition internal combustion engine works.

Explaining something does not mean debunking it or explaining it away. *Naming* is not the same as *explaining*, either. '*Nature* did it, not God' may seem an escape from religion until we ask what 'Nature' is and receive the reply that 'Nature is everything physical there is.' So Nature – 'everything physical there is', and spelt with a capital N – creates everything physical there is – or does it? Or again, 'Natural selection, not a divine designer, was the sculptor of life.'[R]

Expressions of this kind slide into what, in logic, is called the *fallacy of reification* – confusing a *concept* with an actual object or a cause. Concepts such as 'gravity', 'evolution' and 'nature' are particularly prone to this kind of treatment, being credited with the ability to act as purposive agents. It is all very well jokingly to blame 'gravity' if we drop a plate and break it, or to blame 'entropy' for the untidy state of our room. But it is a serious matter to confuse categories and reify concepts by saying 'It wasn't God; evolution *did* it.'

To summarize, Ockham's razor does not warrant dismissing God's *agency* and substituting a *process* – natural selection – in its place. All natural selection shows is that there is a much simpler explanation of the mechanisms of adaptation (arguably employed by God) than treating each living thing as being separately equipped.

God of the Gaps

Muddling up different *types* of explanation has a long history and has led to the fallacy of the God of the Gaps. Unnecessarily anxious theologians once thought God was being pushed out by an increase in scientific knowledge. They adopted the strategy of saying 'You scientists may have explained "X" but you haven't explained "Y" – that's God.' They 'plugged God in' where there were currently no satisfactory scientific explanations.

Apart from being a philosophical confusion, this was a counterproductive and retreating position that would inevitably lead to people thinking God was 'squeezed out of the gaps' by science – just as the atheist would wish! Dawkins expresses astonishment at those who see 'natural selection as "God's way of achieving his creation" '.[118] No astonishment is appropriate if the foregoing points have been understood. So you can take your pick as to whether you call the muddle the 'God of the Gaps' or the 'Infinitely Lazy Creator' of Professor Peter Atkins, whom both Atkins and Dawkins see as ending up with nothing to do if evolution *did it*!

God of the Gaps views God as a valid replacement for missing scientific explanations.

Gap of a God

But here we are confronted with something like an atheistic converse of the God of the Gaps. This is the belief that *scientific* explanations oust explanations of the *agency* of God, which I shall call Gap of a God. It is one of the most major misunderstandings about the interplay between science and religion and is frequently employed to bolster up the 'conflict thesis' about science and religion.

Gap of a God views scientific explanations as valid replacements for God.

A conundrum

The importance of recognizing the plurality of explanations brings with it a puzzle and a philosophical snare. We often feel frustrated when something is baffling and unexplained. So our psychological needs for release may be met simply by supplying a label – the naming/explaining fallacy. Why do bodies fall?

Gravity! How does this work? Computers! There may also be a connection between failing to recognize that there can be different types of compatible explanations and this tendency to be satisfied with any *one* type of explanation. If it relieves a sense of frustration, other valid types of explanation, which also need to be taken into account, may be overlooked.

Where do we draw the boundary?

A7 'Religion is a scientific theory.'[1]

'I pay religions the compliment of regarding them as scientific theories.'[2]

'I shall suggest that the existence of God is a scientific hypothesis.'[50]

The first two claims are not recent but seem consistent with the third and three similar ones in *The God Delusion*.[2, 50, 105] But is it coherent to expect a scientific test for God, who is not a material object? Would any professional philosopher support such a view? The scientific enterprise, by its subject matter of material things and by its methods, does not concern itself with First Causes. They lie outside of science's remit, allowing those of all faiths, and of none, to work together in a worthwhile enterprise. So there is something odd about turning to science, the study of the natural world, in the hope of answering religious questions about whether there is anything *other* than the natural world (that is, God) to which the natural world owes its existence. This raises questions about where the boundary lies between science and non-science – the matter of demarcation.

Demarcation

Philosophers, using rather precise language, speak about science and about religion as each belonging to a different 'universe of discourse', by which they mean something like an 'area of enquiry' or 'field of study'. Each is 'a system of concepts and entities related to a particular topic or area of interest, within which certain terms and expressions acquire their own meaning or significance'.[3]

In more homely language, science, religion and ethics each have their special terms or concepts, with specific meanings within that area of study. 'Work', 'power' and 'energy' have different meanings in physics from their meanings in everyday life. 'Reinforcement' means one thing in psychology and something different in war studies. Science has concepts such as mass, velocity, species, electron and alkali, while religion has concepts such as God, spirit and resurrection. Ethics is constituted by concepts such as obligation, right and wrong. But we don't expect to encounter 'God-talk' in science or 'chromosomes' in religion.

All this seems fairly straightforward, but to claim that God's existence is a scientific hypothesis seems a hybrid that confuses the concepts and procedures of science and religion. Dawkins seems to offer two main reasons for his surprising view. First, that there would be a scientifically detectable difference in a universe with a creator and one without [55, 61], and second, that if God communicated with his creatures that would involve science.[154]

The key to understanding Dawkins' position seems to lie in identifying his concept of God. Initially he set himself the ambitious agenda of 'attacking God, all gods, anything and everything supernatural'.[36] Then he sees that a very simple view of God needs to be 'fleshed out if it is to accommodate the Abrahamic God. He not only created the universe; he is a personal God.'[38]

The Judeo-Christian concept of God

This, though necessarily employing anthropomorphic terms – for what else could be used? – is not of some kind of larger-than-life, created being with embodied memory in multi-gigabytes. It is of an eternal being that is most appropriately spoken of in personal language; the creator (bringer into being) and sustainer (maintainer in being) of everything there is. Some theologians prefer to bring both ideas together under the umbrella term 'creation'. Unbounded by time or space, both of which are of God's creation and upholding, creation is a timeless *act*, independent of any particular mechanisms. It is not the same thing as the Big Bang. The latter, cosmologists believe, marks the physical beginning of our universe some 13.7 thousand million (10^9) years ago when time and space came into being. The Earth itself is about 4.6×10^9 years old. Furthermore, although God is *immanent* within creation, God is also *transcendent*.

To ask the question 'Who made God?' is to reveal a misunderstanding of the concept of the Judaeo-Christian God. If any 'Being' had 'created God', that Being would be God. 'Created gods are, by definition, a delusion.'[4] So the appropriate comment on Dawkins' first reason for claiming religion to be a scientific hypothesis is that the absence of a 'creative superintendent'[55] or 'original guiding agent'[61] would not mean a different kind of universe but no universe at all.

With regard to the second reason, Dawkins speculates on the 'bandwidth' needed for the information transfer between God and humans, figuring that God 'must have something far more elaborately and non-randomly constructed than the largest brain or the largest computer we know'.[154] But God is not a 'constructed' Being, and unless Dawkins' 'construction' involved something physical, it would not be accessible to science anyway.

The nature of science
Dawkins' view of science seems to indicate an over-estimation of its scope, reminiscent of the positivism and logical positivism of the late nineteenth and first half of the twentieth centuries. That Golden Image of science, with its all-embracing claims as the final authority on every claim to truth, fell foul of its own Verification Principle, because the principle could not itself be verified scientifically – another example of the *reflexivity* principle of Chapter 3. It shot itself in the

foot and because its feet were of clay, they shattered.[5] The Image toppled and logical positivism was finally abandoned by its champion, Professor A. J. Ayer. The downsized reconstruction of science is all the healthier for a realistic recognition of its limitations as well as its huge strengths. If, however, as Dawkins asserts, atheists believe that nothing exists except the physical world (p. 21), and the subject matter of science *is* the material world, then an overestimation of science's scope and capability must be a constant temptation.

One problem with Dawkins' position is the impression it may convey about the nature of science. Here it is inextricably muddled up with Dawkins' personal beliefs in atheism and in a conflict between science and religion. This gives science an undeservedly bad name. By contrast, another biologist, Professor Francis Collins, leader of the Human Genome Project, can say, 'for me the experience of sequencing the human genome, and uncovering this most remarkable of all texts, was both a stunning scientific achievement and an occasion of worship'.[6]

At a time when recruitment to scientific careers does not meet demand, the last thing we need is to have religious believers discouraged from science because these two aspects of life are portrayed as incompatible. Regrettably, some of the reasons for this polarized view have been generated from within a section of the religious community itself. Its mid-twentieth-century disinterring of beliefs in a geologically young Earth, part of 'young-Earth' creation*ism,* has not helped at all. This has resurfaced despite the verdict of historians of science such as Professor David Livingstone that 'by and large, Christian geologists had both encountered and accommodated the issue of the age of the earth long before the appearance of Darwin's theory'.[7]

Studying science is a highly worthwhile career and many religious believers have engaged in it. Historically, this is reflected by the so-called 'Research Workers' Text' from Psalm 111:2 over the doors of both the original and the new Cavendish laboratories in Cambridge. Translated, it reads, 'The works of the Lord are great, sought out of all them that have pleasure therein.' Many of the founder members of the Royal Society, founded in 1660, were themselves in Holy Orders.

Peter Harrison, Andreas Idreos Professor of Science and Religion at Oxford University, writes:

> **Those who argue for the incompatibility of science and religion will draw little comfort from history... Those who have magnified more recent controversies about the relations of science and religion, and projected them back into historical time, simply perpetuate a historical myth... the myth of a perennial conflict between science and religion is one to which no historian of science would subscribe.[8]**

Similar comments by five other professors of the history of science are reproduced in my *User's Guide to Science and Belief.*[9]

Certain branches of the media have helped, unintentionally or intentionally, to perpetuate this 'historical myth'. Confrontation is spicy and good for viewing ratings. There are exceptions, but, on the whole, too many television programmes portray anachronistic views of science-and-religion. At a conference of historians of science, a science correspondent replied to delegates' criticism of a broadcast programme. Faulted on a historical matter, the correspondent replied to the effect, 'Oh well, it made a good story.' The historians were not impressed. In anticipation of media confusions about Darwin's own views on religion and science, in the year of celebrating the 200th anniversary of Darwin's birth and the 150th anniversary of the 1859 publication of *The Origin of Species,* a useful article was put online.[10] Entitled 'Charles Darwin on Religion', it was written by a historian of science and religion, Professor John Hedley Brooke, currently President of the International Society for Science and Religion and Peter Harrison's predecessor in the Andreas Idreos Chair.

To conclude with 'the God Hypothesis', where we began, Dawkins considers it is unnecessary in any of its forms. He footnotes the much repeated '"Sire, I had no need of that hypothesis," as Laplace said…'[46] A conversation with a Professor of the History of Science indicates that there is no known written evidence that Laplace ever said these words.

8

An endangered species?

A8 '... good scientists who are sincerely religious in the full, traditional sense', both in the United States and in Britain, 'stand out for their rarity and are a subject of amused bafflement to their peers in the academic community.'[99]

If science is elevated beyond its station and portrayed as anti-religion, it is not to be expected that scientists with religious beliefs will be highly regarded. Nevertheless, it has not been obvious to me, during forty years of teaching in a university, that Christian colleagues were being treated with this 'amused bafflement'.

Eleven seconds say a lot

On the TV programme *Heart of the Matter* of 29 September 1996, Richard Dawkins spoke with Professor Jim Watson, one of the discoverers of the double-helical structure of DNA. In *The God Delusion*,

Dawkins recounts their brief meeting:

In 1996... I interviewed my friend Jim Watson... I asked Watson whether he knew many religious scientists today. He replied: 'Virtually none. Occasionally I meet them, and I'm a bit embarrassed [laughs] because, you know, I can't believe anyone accepts truth by revelation.'[99]

As a result of the impression given that scientists who held religious beliefs were odd, ten scientists were invited to write 250 words each on their Christian faith and their scientific studies. The ten contributors were:

- **R. J. (Sam) Berry FRSE**, Professor of Genetics, England
- **Sir Robert Boyd FRS**, Professor of Physics and Astronomy, England
- **Owen Gingerich**, Professor of Astronomy and the History of Science, United States
- **Margaret Hodson**, Professor of Respiratory Medicine, England
- **Sir John Houghton FRS**, formerly Professor of Atmospheric Physics, Wales
- **Malcolm Jeeves FRSE**, Professor of Psychology, Scotland
- **Gareth Jones**, Professor of Anatomy and Structural Biology, New Zealand
- **George Kinoti**, Professor of Zoology, Africa
- **Sir Ghillean Prance FRS**, Professor of Botany, England
- **Colin Russell**, Professor of History of Science and Technology, England.

Some of these contributions to *God and the Scientists*

can be seen on the Christians in Science website.[1] Eighteen lengthier contributions are published in *Real Scientists, Real Faith*.[2]

Dawkins' views on scientists with religious beliefs

Dawkins considers that great scientists who seem religious 'become harder to find through the twentieth century, but they are not particularly rare'. The apparent contradiction between not being 'particularly rare' and standing out for 'their rarity' in A8 (above) arises because the first comment applies to what Dawkins calls the 'Einsteinian sense', which he distinguishes from 'supernatural religion' and considers to be a misapplication of the word 'religious'. Flew takes him to task about Einstein, saying, 'Richard Dawkins propounds my old view that Einstein was an atheist. In doing so, Dawkins ignores Einstein's categorical statement [cited] above that he was neither an atheist nor a pantheist.' Flew gives a detailed rebuttal of this view.[3]

A touch of humour?

Dawkins goes on to say

> Nevertheless there are some genuine specimens of good scientists who are sincerely religious in the full, traditional sense. Among contemporary British scientists, the same three names crop up with the likeable familiarity of senior partners in a firm of Dickensian lawyers: Peacocke, Stannard and Polkinghorne.[99]

But after three similar references to these three scientists the repetitions began to seem tedious and misleading. They make scientists who are Christians sound like an endangered species. The use of the word 'specimens' makes them appear even more like collector's pieces, giving the impression that such people are quaint, archaic and a generation on the verge of extinction. This is far from the case. The late Revd Dr Arthur Peacocke was an Oxford researcher on DNA and sometime Dean of Clare College, Cambridge; Professor Russell Stannard was head of the physics department at the Open University; and Revd Dr John Polkinghorne was professor of mathematical physics at Cambridge. There is nothing 'Dickensian' about any of them: men of razor-sharp minds and prolific academic outputs, both in science and in the relationships between science and religion.

Is this a species under threat?

Dawkins continues to express his views about scientists with religious beliefs, saying, 'The efforts of apologists to find genuinely distinguished modern scientists who are religious have an air of desperation, generating the unmistakably hollow sounds of bottoms of barrels being scraped.'[100] I find this statement surprising. Not only are there many scientists who have religious interests, but many such academics have formed societies to engage in scholarly studies of, and produce publications about, the interplay between science and religion. The following figures of membership numbers in a few of these societies were collected around 2007:

- International Society for Science & Religion (modelled on the lines of the Royal Society) – 150
- The European Society for the Study of Science and Theology – 250
- The Institute for the Study of Christianity in an Age of Science and Technology (Australia) – 45 Fellows and 156 associates
- Christians in Science (UK) – 770
- Science and Religion Forum (UK) – 350
- American Scientific Affiliation – 2,000 members, associates, friends and subscribers (numbers may be inflated as they include 'friends' and 'subscribers').

These figures do not, of course, represent the unnumbered body of scientists with religious beliefs, but a sample of those who are fascinated enough to engage in serious study, debate and, in many cases, publishing in this area. Academic study of the relationships between science and religion has become quite an industry in the last couple of decades. Learned societies have grown numerically and, throughout the world, over 700 undergraduate and postgraduate courses on science and religion have been kick-started through grants administered by the Center for Theology and the Natural Sciences in the United States.

Without these facts and figures, the impression left by Dawkins' book might have been that such people are rare.

9

Back to the drawing board – but whose?

A9 'Darwin has removed the main argument for God's existence.'[1]

The final two chapters will consider 'the central argument'[157] of Dawkins' book which sets out to explain the origin of the universe's apparent design without invoking actual design.

Darwin's theory

William Paley, the eighteenth-century mathematician and theologian, imagined finding a watch, designed for a purpose, on a heath. He argued, by analogy, that creatures apparently fitted for their environment also pointed to a designer. Not all Paley's contemporaries accepted his arguments. Darwin, at first impressed by Paley's writings, later wrote:

> **The old argument from design in Nature, as given by Paley, which formerly seemed to me so conclusive, fails, now that the law of natural selection has been discovered.**[2]

Darwin knew that offspring inherited characteristics from their parents, suggesting that characteristics favourable to survival and reproduction would be preserved. He called the processes *natural selection* by comparison with the *artificial selection* practised by racehorse breeders and others.

Darwin's theory altered Paley's form of an argument for God from design but did not remove the idea of design altogether. Darwin suggested that the design lay in the laws God created – 'the Creator creates by... laws' – commenting that 'I can see no reason why a man, or other animal, may not have been expressly designed by an omniscient Creator, who foresaw every future event and consequence.'[3]

Design – actual or only apparent?

So, could the 'appearance of design' in nature have resulted from 'actual design'? Suppose God creates a universe involving a Big Bang. High-energy particles in stars, building up the heavier elements for life, are moving randomly. 'Chance' processes are involved, using the word not in its popular sense of 'accidental', which implies lack of intention, but in a technical meaning of 'unpredictable'.

If it seems odd that God might employ 'chance processes' in a designed universe, we should remember that intelligent beings of the human variety now use 'chance' and 'selection' in design. They use computers, mimicking the processes of reproduction in biology, in sophisticated programs called *genetic algorithms*[4] to solve optimization problems such as 'the best shape for this' or 'the best place for that'. Indeed, before these sophisticated techniques became common, Dawkins spoke of 'Darwinian design' in connection with using 'chance' and 'selection' procedures to produce efficient aerofoil sections.[5] In the second of his Christmas lectures he referred to this again, saying that the aerofoil designer 'claims that he designs his windmills by a kind of natural selection'.[6]

To continue the story, those high-energy particles collided and fused together to transform the primitive constituents of the early universe into the rich variety of material that is all around us. Later, at much reduced energy, when living organisms appeared, the residue of these particles and radiation would produce mutations. After the 'chance' mutations, which change the DNA, 'selection' leads to the survival of 'fitter' offspring. The mutations result in the astonishing diversity of life, but also in cancers and seemingly unpleasant creatures like the wasp-like Ichneumonidæ, about which Darwin corresponded with a Christian colleague, Professor Asa Gray. Darwin wrote, 'I am bewildered. I had no intention to write atheistically... I cannot persuade myself that a beneficent and omnipotent God would have designedly created the Ichneumonidæ with the express intention of their feeding within the living bodies of caterpillars.'[7] Such things are often cited as reasons for denying design, but it may be that these outcomes, rather than being end-products of a divine plan, are inevitable by-products – the cost, if you like – of the processes involved.

By way of illustration, Alfred Nobel did not design dynamite to kill people but to make the unstable explosive nitroglycerine safe for industrial use in blasting rock. Its unintended use in war, to which he reacted in horror, prompted him to create a Peace Prize. By contrast, napalm was *designed* to stick to things, including human flesh, and to burn, resulting in an excruciating death.

The presence of consequences unintended (but not unforeseen) by God does not, however, rule out divine design, even though Dawkins claims that 'natural objects... have imperfections which you wouldn't expect to get in objects designed by a real designer'.[8] This doesn't follow if God's creative activity produced a world by the processes we are familiar with. Once something is created, certain other things follow.

Unintended consequences can be further illustrated by the theist's belief that 'love' is an intended feature of the universe. For this, free will has to be part of the 'package', even though evil deeds will result from human choices. C. S. Lewis points out that

> **It is no more possible for God than for the weakest of his creatures to carry out both of two mutually exclusive alternatives; not because His power meets an obstacle, but because nonsense remains nonsense even when we talk it about God.**[9]

More recently, and more concisely, Flew observes that 'you cannot limit the possibilities of omnipotence except to produce the logically impossible'.[10]

It would be nice if all, and only, photons of radiation leading to cancerous mutations were made to fizzle out. It would be great if every bullet fired in anger turned to jelly. But the strength of steel that provides safe railway bridges also permits guns and fatal stabbings.

In the thirteenth century, Alfonso X of Castile, who had scientific interests in astronomy, is reported as saying, 'If the Lord Almighty had consulted me before embarking upon Creation, I should have recommended something simpler.' But there has been a noticeable lack of any such recommendations of practical alternatives for bringing about our world!

An 'automatic' process?

There is another way in which the idea of design could be preserved. Instead of God designing everything separately so that each was individually adapted to its environment, natural selection could be seen as a much more economical way for God to achieve the adaptation of living things automatically to their respective environments. By analogy, when electric street lights were invented they had to be turned on and off by hand. In January 1955, industrial smoke trapped under a cloud caused total darkness in London in the middle of the day, since at that time there were no photoelectric detectors on street lamps to turn them on automatically when the daylight failed. Had there been, the lamps would have responded automatically to the environmental change.

Making a similar point about the living world, Darwin, in *The Origin of Species*, quoted with approval a letter he received from Revd Professor Charles Kingsley:

A celebrated author and divine has written to me that 'he has gradually learnt to see that it is just as noble a conception of the Deity to believe that He created a few original forms capable of self-development into other

and needful forms, as to believe that He required a fresh act of creation to supply the voids caused by the action of His laws'.[11]

Frederick Temple, later to become Archbishop of Canterbury, commented similarly:

What is touched by this doctrine [of evolution] is not the evidence of design but the mode in which the design was executed... In the one case the Creator made the animals at once such as they now are; in the other case He impressed on certain particles of matter... such inherent powers that in the ordinary course of time living creatures such as the present were developed... He did not make the things, we may say; no, but He made them make themselves.[12]

Evolution by natural selection involves processes for automatically transmitting characteristics favourable to survival and reproduction, resulting in *adaption* to environments where predation, limited food and restricted space are present.

According to the first chapter of Genesis, the created order is 'good' – that is, 'fit for purpose', having an inbuilt capability to function. Mark's Gospel contains a classic passage which illustrates this, while obviously not denying the underlying activity of God:

A man scatters seed on the ground... the seed sprouts and grows, though he does not know how. All by itself [Greek *automatos*] the soil produces corn – first the stalk, then the ear, then the full grain in the ear (4:26–28).

Failure to recognize the *functional integrity of creation*[13] has encouraged the muddle of the God of the Gaps encountered in Chapter 6.

A bad argument, but not by atheists

In the early 1990s the Intelligent Design (ID) Movement was founded in America, arguing that:

- some living things are so irreducibly complex that a single missing part would stop the organism functioning;
- such organisms could not have arisen by the normal evolutionary processes;
- they must therefore have been designed by an (unnamed) intelligence – generally understood as God.

Their examples of irreducible complexity include the human blood-clotting cascade, the immune system, the bacterial flagellum – a minute propeller that moves certain bacteria – and the human eye. In *River out of Eden*, Dawkins gives a brilliant account of the evolutionary development of the eye, at least forty times, independently.[14]

There are difficulties about the ID Movement's biology, logic and theology. What happens if an organism, taken to exhibit irreducible complexity, is later found to have an evolutionary explanation? (This has since happened with blood-clotting and the immune system.) Does that mean the organism no longer points to an Intelligent Designer?

ID supporters overlook how intermediate organisms in the evolutionary process may fulfil different functions from later ones, rendering their complex mathematical arguments wrong. To illustrate this point, Dawkins quotes a nice metaphor about how the construction of an arch of stones usually needs scaffolding which afterwards can be taken away. He uses the metaphor to illustrate the disappearance of some earlier part of the evolutionary process which gave rise to the current organism.

But what about organisms that do not show irreducible complexity? Doesn't everything show God's handiwork, as the Abrahamic religions Christianity, Islam and Judaism believe? Although ID theorists do not deny this, that is the direction in which their logic leads. The more science finds natural explanations, the less room there appears to be for God's activity! Richard Dawkins is right to point out that this involves a classic example of the God of the Gaps.[128] It has resulted in an own goal for its followers. Despite this, the traditional arguments for design are not affected by ID's poor argument. Incidentally, the word 'design' presupposes intelligence, so making the word 'intelligent' redundant.

ID is distinct from, though often confused with, (young-Earth) creationism. Creationism creates a similar linguistic problem. Its abbreviated label, being barely distinguishable from the traditional word 'creation', muddies the waters still further. Some well-argued lectures on evolution end up by dismissing creationism in a few words at the end, without distinguishing it from traditional beliefs in creation. It is only the 'young-Earth' part that goes. Thus a second own goal may arise if others who rightly reject a young Earth, illegitimately portray it as justifying the rejection of creation also.

Conclusion

Dawkins wrote in *The Blind Watchmaker* that 'although atheism might have been logically tenable before Darwin, Darwin made it possible to be an intellectually fulfilled atheist'.[15] But atheism – the denial of God – is not entailed by discovering the *mechanisms* of biological adaptation. As indicated in Chapter 6, this confuses two different types of explanation, concerning, respectively, *agency* and *mechanisms*. Dawkins' belief that evolution is the only alternative to 'ultimate design' involves a *category mistake*. Once life has arisen, evolution provides a scientific explanation of the *adaptation* of living things to their environments. It can tell us nothing about pre-biotic states, nor whether God is responsible for the processes involved.

In short, evolution is a broken crutch for supporting atheism.

Unpeeling the cosmic onion

A10 '… some kind of multiverse theory could in principle do for physics the same explanatory work as Darwin does for biology'[158], rendering God improbable.

'… any God capable of designing anything would have to be complex enough to demand the same kind of explanation in his own right. God presents an infinite regress.'[109]

Universe or multiverse?

William of Ockham would doubtless approve of considering a universe before a multiverse![1] In the 1970s it became apparent that if there were miniscule differences in several physical constants, carbon-based 'life as we know it' would not have arisen. According to Professor Stephen Hawking, a minute increase of about one part in a million million in the density of the universe one second after the Big Bang would have meant a recollapse of the universe after some ten years. A similar decrease in density would have resulted in a largely empty universe after the same time.[2]

In neither scenario would the stars, necessary to cook up the elements for life over some billions of years, have formed. In a rapidly expanding universe, this time span has resulted in the universe being enormous. But if it were not so big, so old, so dark and so cold, we would not be here. The apparent suitability of our universe for life is addressed in what is called the *Anthropic Cosmological Principle*. This consists of two parts, which need to be kept distinct.

The *anthropic principle* (Greek *anthropos*, man/humanity – though all life is included) involves speculation about the possible role of humans in the universe. For instance, are humans an inevitable outcome of the structure of the universe? More enigmatically, are they the necessary observers that the Copenhagen interpretation of quantum mechanics seems to require to bring the universe about? Some of these discussions are very complicated and need not detain us here.

Fortunately, the *anthropic coincidences* are much easier to understand. From experimental observations, it seems that certain constants of nature appear to have been 'fine-tuned' for life as we know it to have arisen. So does this apparent fine-tuning imply some kind of cosmic designer? Certainly it seems to be a candidate for a modern version of a design argument, though it might only point towards a super-intelligence and not necessarily to the Judaeo-Christian God. These cosmic coincidences have prompted the label the

Goldilocks effect because, as with Baby Bear's bed, chair and porridge, things are 'just right'.

Dawkins' makes a puzzling assertion that 'the anthropic principle, like natural selection, is an *alternative*'[136] to any form of design and 'is only ever mentioned in the context of the problem that it solves, namely that we live in a life-friendly place. What the religious mind then fails to grasp is that two candidate solutions are offered to the problem. God is one. The anthropic principle is the other.'[136]

But what Dawkins refers to as the 'anthropic principle' (more exactly, the *anthropic coincidences*) is not simply our living in a place that is friendly to life. True, our position in orbit round our Sun, together with our extensive oceans, means Earth's temperature remains somewhere between about ±50°C, making it 'life-friendly'. Furthermore, water's maximum density at 4°C means that ice forms on the tops of ponds, which helps preserve aquatic life in cold weather. But all this was known long before the term 'anthropic principle' was coined in 1974. Anthropic coincidences mean not simply favourable conditions *for life surviving* but the very preconditions *of life arising* in the first place. This would not have happened if various factors about the natural world had been different, including infinitesimal differences in the fundamental constants of nature. So surely his 'life-friendly' should read 'life-conducive'.

Enter the multiverse

The whole idea of multiple universes, instead of just one, is very difficult to envisage, but it goes something like this. In the very early stages of the Big Bang, it is thought that the universe underwent a 'brief' period (10^{-32} seconds!) of rapid expansion – an inflationary phase – to the size of a small grapefruit. In this miniscule period it is *suggested* that many different 'cosmic domains' *might* have arisen in which the constants of nature *may* have been different.

Cosmologists who have studied these early moments have worked on quantum gravity and quantum cosmology because the sizes involved in those primordial moments were so tiny that quantum effects were significant. This makes the whole cosmic picture much more fuzzy and speculative. If multitudes, perhaps infinite numbers, of 'cosmic domains' are spawned off, each of which *might* become separate, incommunicable regions of space–time with different physical constants, the attraction of this multiverse scenario for atheism is obvious. *Maybe* every possible set of physical constants is realized, so at least one has the properties for life to emerge.

Note the italicized words, *suggested, might, may* and *maybe*. Although a multiverse is a possibility to entertain, much of the discussion is speculative metaphysics, so it is premature for confident assertions such as 'I believe in a multiverse.' On present understanding, there could be no communication between these cosmic domains, so it appears that other universes could not be detected from our own. Consequently, whereas it may be theoretically possible, it is presently untestable. So could such a theory be classed as 'scientific'? Furthermore, is it explaining the world in the most economic way? Critics of some atheists' enthusiasm for a multiverse suggest it is the supreme disregard of Ockham's razor to postulate anything up to an infinite number of universes to avoid any suggestion of a single universe designed by God!

Now the only way in which part of Dawkins' contentious statement (above) could seem to make sense would be if he had already committed himself to belief in a multiverse. But this would sit uneasily with his insistence on scientific evidence for anything he believes, because other cosmic domains in a multiverse appear to be detached from the observations on which anything to be classed as scientific depends.

Mind-boggling!

Trying to envisage a multiverse stretches our mental powers to the uttermost, although that does not rule it out, for much of science is counter-intuitive. So would this help? A child had a toy carpet-sweeper. A picture on it showed a child pushing an identical toy carpet-sweeper and on that carpet-sweeper a tiny spot could be seen which was presumably a picture of a child pushing a carpet-sweeper. Fascinating! Would the sequence go on for ever – in grown-up talk, an infinite regress? But where did those other children live? Could they communicate with the others, who seemed to live in different worlds? Was this that child's earliest hint of a carpet-sweeper multiverse? One thing was clear, however: the child never expected to come across the carpet-sweeper's inventor.

The idea of a necessary choice between a multiverse or God is another example of the fallacy of the excluded middle, encountered in Chapter 3. The arising of our particular domain within a multiverse would no more disprove divine activity than natural selection disproves divine activity in organic adaptation, the conclusion of the previous chapter. To speculate further, multiple universes might show God's creative activity to be far greater than it was thought. It might even be the case that if the inflationary phase referred to could *not* have given rise to cosmic domains, resulting in a multiverse, then it couldn't have given rise to our own. The potential for other domains to arise might be a necessary scenario for our own to exist.

Probability

Dawkins' claims about the improbability of God appeal to two separate lines of thought. The first is a statistical one; the second is an infinite regress. He calls 'the statistical demonstration that God almost certainly does not exist ... the Ultimate Boeing 747 gambit'.[113] He explains the scientist Fred Hoyle's view that the probability that life would arise on Earth was comparable to that of a hurricane, blowing through a scrapyard, assembling a Boeing 747. Dawkins goes on to say, 'However statistically improbable the entity you seek to explain by invoking a designer, the designer himself has got to be at least as improbable. God is the Ultimate Boeing 747.'[114]

The argument appears flawed on two grounds. The improbability about the Boeing 747 lies in its being assembled that way. But an eternal God is not a physical object, to be assembled. Dawkins' argument is an analogical one, passing from some kind of physical entity to the non-existence of a non-physical God. But this is a type of analogical argument he rejects when applied to our world having a designer God because physical artefacts have designers.

Second, the word 'statistical' is inappropriate in arguing about the existence of God, something that could be illustrated with reference to the idea of a multiverse. Suppose we had grounds for being certain about a multiverse, and also knew that a very small fraction of these universes, or cosmic domains, were created by 'God'. Then we might justifiably infer that, for *our* universe, God was 'statistically improbable'. That is the only valid way terms like 'statistical demonstration' and 'statistically improbable' could be used.[113f.]

So, if the concept of probability is to be introduced, more moderate claims seem called for. 'Probability' might be used in an everyday sense to mean 'what seems likely with present knowledge and understanding'. If so, one general way of deciding probability would be to take the 'pointers' to God's existence, outlined in Chapter 4, and evaluate how far they support a *cumulative case* for God.

Design and infinite regress

Dawkins attempts to rebut the idea of design by maintaining that it leads to an infinite regress, as in the second statement of A10 (above).

So let's take a look at the idea of a regress:

• Every particle of carbon in our bodies was formed

in a distant star some thousands of millions of years ago.

- The carbon resulted from lighter particles colliding and fusing together within 'nuclear reactors' called stars.
- Stars formed as gravitational attraction drew material together, generating heat.
- Material 'condensed out' from a Big Bang as the temperature dropped.

All these explanations are, to use William of Ockham's words, 'of the same kind': physical explanations, with no mention of God. There is no obvious indication that the sequence, like the unpeeling of some cosmic onion, is an infinite regress. Strange behaviour occurs at very small times and lengths where quantum effects become significant, such as 'the Planck time' (10^{-43} seconds) and the 'Planck length' (10^{-33} cm)'. The latter is the smallest quantity having the dimensions of length that can result from the three fundamental constants of nature, namely, Newton's gravitational constant, the velocity of light and Planck's constant. Leaving aside the details, every smaller unpacking is still expressed in physical quantities. When the last layer of wrapping paper – or onion – is removed, we don't find God.

Summing up, it is questionable whether there *is* a physical infinite regress within our universe. But whichever way the answer lies, it has little bearing on the flawed 'Who made God?' argument. The idea of 'being made' is conceptually excluded in the case of the Judaeo-Christian God, as indicated in Chapter 7.

Second, an argument from infinite regress

founders, since its use of 'before' makes it only applicable in time. An expression 'before time began' has no meaning – except as a literary device to try to express the inexpressible – any more than the ancient theological question 'What was God doing before he created the world?' makes sense. Without time, there is no 'before'. While not denying God's eternal existence, this is lethal to the 'infinite regress' argument.

Summary

Taking the incalculable number of deeds done in connection with religion beliefs, and selecting only the nasty ones, is not a good argument for arriving at the verdict that 'religion is bad'. Neither is an idiosyncratic portrayal of faith as 'unevidenced belief' a valid way of dismissing religious faith. Despite a denial, the word 'faith' is also used in ordinary speech by atheists. This prompted an inspection in Chapter 3 of a further six ways in which particular words have been employed against religious believers, revealing that the accusing finger, on closer inspection, has four additional fingers pointing backwards to the hand's owner.

On examining the matter of evidence more closely, it can be rationally concluded that the different types of evidence provide adequate grounds for a cumulative case for belief – and trust – in God. Criticisms of the biblical records, as one of the types of evidence, were judged to be far too superficial and dismissive to be convincing or to do justice to the writings themselves and the scholars who have studied them.

Different *types* of evidence, however, point to different types of explanation. An apparent lack of understanding of this point highlights *a* – if not *the* – major confusion which has muddied the waters of science/religion debates, namely the idea that scientific explanations oust religious ones. But once the assumption is made that the material world is all there is, certain other beliefs, unsurprisingly, are likely to follow. Science may be seen as providing the ultimate test for truth, best questioned by examining the boundaries of science's competence. The rise and fall of science as a Golden Image is now a distant chapter in the history of recent philosophy. Scientific explanations are not the only valid ones. They are the best ones if we are interested, say, in trying to increase the viability of prematurely born babies, but they are of no help in providing the language of courtship and love that led to the conception in the first place. 'Pair-bonding' is the farthest science can go.

One consequence of regarding science too highly, and as being in opposition to religion, is a corresponding tendency to downplay scientists who practise their religion in parallel with their scientific careers. The facts and figures show, however, that there is rather more activity within *academia* on relating science to religion than some atheists seem aware.

This led to examining the main argument of Dawkins' book in the last two chapters. His all too common assertion that evolutionary processes of adaptation replace the idea of God's agency involves a category mistake, confusing the explanation of a *process* with a different type of explanation – the *act* of an agent. It is also an example of the fallacy of the excluded middle, since it is *coherent* to regard evolution as part of God's creative process and not necessary to have to choose between them. A similar fallacy is evident in the suggestion that a multiverse might eliminate a designing God. Also rejected are further attempts, arguing along probability and infinite regress lines, to banish what turns out in the end to be a highly anthropomorphic 'god'.

Many of the assertions made appeared to be

inadequately supported by arguments. Such arguments as *are* offered don't seem to hold water. Supremely, the edifice of atheism that Dawkins and many others have attempted to construct from evolution has been erected on inappropriate and insecure foundations, ones which are quite unable to bear the weight of the superstructure.

So, apart from being more vociferous, what's new about the 'New Atheism'? This question, posed at the outset, is itself also the answer, albeit in a different tone of voice: 'What's new?'

Bendy-bus theology

On London's 'bendy buses', early in 2009, there appeared the slogan 'There's probably no God. Now stop worrying and enjoy life.' 'Probably' is a word that seems to feature quite a lot in the literature of atheism. Dawkins would have preferred 'almost certainly'.

That particular slogan prompts one final question. If God has the same status as tooth fairies and Father Christmas, as Dawkins appears to think, is it necessary to spend so much money trying to persuade people that God doesn't exist?

Notes

About this book

1. Various academic colleagues have given more detailed and scholarly responses than I have been able to attempt in this brief space. See McGrath, A., *Dawkins' God: Genes, Memes and the Meaning of Life,* Oxford: Blackwell, 2005 (now translated into twelve languages); and Ward, K., *God, Chance & Necessity,* Oxford: Oneworld Publications, 1996, and *Why There Almost Certainly Is a God,* Oxford: Lion Hudson, 2008. I have, however, given other, lengthier treatments in my *User's Guide to Science and Belief,* Oxford: Lion Hudson, 2007.

2. Converting people from one set of beliefs to another.

3. Gray, J., 'The Atheist Delusion', *The Guardian,* Saturday 15 March 2008.

4. Flew, A., *There Is a God,* New York: HarperCollins, 2007.

5. Flew, A., *God and Philosophy*, London: Hutchinson, 1974, p. 141.

Chapter 1

1. Channel 4, 9 and 10 January 2006.

2. BBC Radio Merseyside, 10 January 2006.

3. *Science: The National Curriculum for England,* London: Department for Education and Employment/Qualifications and Curriculum Authority, 2006, p. 37.

Chapter 2

1. Grayling, A. C., 'Religions don't deserve special treatment', *The Guardian,* Thursday 19 October 2006.

2. A year to the day before the legendary encounter of Bishop Samuel Wilberforce with Thomas Henry Huxley in Oxford.

Chapter 3

1. Dawkins, R., *The Selfish Gene,* Oxford: Oxford University Press, 1976, p. 192.

2. Dawkins, p. 192.

3. Dawkins, p. 198.

4. Dawkins, p. 193.

5. Dawkins, R., *A Devil's Chaplain,* London: Weidenfeld & Nicolson, 2003, p. 137.

6. Dawkins, R., *The Selfish Gene,* p. 193.

7. The subsequent debate between the author and Richard Dawkins can be seen at:

http://www/scienceandchristianbelief.org/articles/dawkinspoole.1.php

http://www.scienceandchristianbelief.org/articles/dawkinspoole2.php

http://www.scienceandchristianbelief.org/articles/dawkinspoole3.php

Chapter 4

1. Adler, M. J., *How to Think about God,* New York: Macmillan, 1980, p.150.

2. Montgomery, J. W., 'A Lawyer's Defence of Christianity', *Faith & Thought,* Vol. 24 (1998), p. 3.

3. Flew, A., *There Is a God,* p. 95.

4. Flew, p. 1.

5. Flew, p. 73.

6. Flew, p. 89.

7. Flew, pp. 88f.

8. Flew, p. 185.

9. Darwin, F. (ed.), *The Autobiography of Charles and Selected Letters,* New York: Dover, 1958, p. 65.

10. St Augustine, *The Literal Meaning of Genesis,* Vol. 1 (trans. J.H. Taylor), New York: Paulist Press, pp. 42f.

11. Flew, A., 'Theology and Falsification' in Flew, A. and MacIntyre, A. (eds), *New Essays in Philosophical Theology,* London: SCM Press, 1955, p. 99.

12. Colossians 1:15–17 and Hebrews 1:1–3.

13. Morison, F., *Who Moved the Stone?,* London: Faber & Faber, 1930, pp. 9, 11f.

14. Morison, F., *Who Moved the Stone?*, Preface.

15. Greenleaf, S., *The Testimony of the Evangelists: The Gospels Examined by the Rules of Evidence Administrated in Courts of Justice* (fifth printing), Grand Rapids: Kregel, 1999, p. 47.

16. Flew, A., *There Is a God*, p. 187.

Chapter 5

1. Humphreys, C. J., 'The Star of Bethlehem', *Quarterly Journal of the Royal Astronomical Society*, Vol. 32 (1991), pp. 389–407, reprinted in *Science and Christian Belief*, Vol. 5 (1993), pp. 83–101 (www.cis.org.uk).

2. Michaels, J. R., *John, New International Bible Commentary*, Carlisle: Paternoster, 1989, pp. 1ff.

3. Humphreys, C. J. and Waddington, W.G., 'Dating the Crucifixion', *Nature*, Vol. 306, No. 5945 (1983), pp. 743–46.

4. Montgomery, J.W., 'A Lawyer's Defence of Christianity', *Faith & Thought*, Vol. 24 (1998), p. 6.

5. Montgomery, J. W., 'A Lawyer's Defence of Christianity', p.4.

6. Bruce, F. F., *The New Testament Documents* (Fifth [revised] edition), London: Inter-Varsity Press, 1970, p. 15.

7. Ives, E. W., *God in History*, Tring: Lion, 1979, p. 18.

8. Bruce, F. F., *The New Testament Documents*, p. 16.

9. Ives, E. W., *God in History*, pp. 18f.

Chapter 7

1. 'A scientist's case against God' – an edited version of Dr Dawkins' speech at the Edinburgh International Science Festival on 15 April 1992, published in *The Independent*, 20 April 1992.

2. Dawkins, R., 'A Reply to Poole', *Science and Christian Belief*, Vol. 7 (1) (1995), p. 46.

3. Flew, A. (editorial consultant), *A Dictionary of Philosophy*, London: Macmillan, 1979, p. 334.

4. John Lennox in debate with Richard Dawkins.

5. For a fuller picture, see my *Beliefs and Values in Science Education*, Buckingham: Open University Press, 1995, Ch. 2, pp. 34–38.

6. Collins, F. S., *The Language of God*, London: Simon &

Schuster, 2007, p. 3.

7. Livingstone, D. N., *Darwin's Forgotten Defenders*, Edinburgh: Scottish Academic Press/Eerdmans, 1987, p. 27.

8. Harrison, P., *Christianity and the Rise of Western Science*, Farmington Paper SC18, Oxford: Farmington Institute for Christian Studies, 2008.

9. Poole, M. W., *User's Guide to Science and Belief*, Oxford: Lion Hudson, 2007, p. 89.

10. http://www.issr.org.uk/darwin-religion.asp. Also published in Brooke, J. H., 'Charles Darwin on Religion', *Perspectives on Science and Christian Faith*, Vol. 62 (2) (2009), pp. 67–72.

Chapter 8

1. http://www.cis.org.uk/resources/articles/general

2. Berry, R. J., *Real Scientists, Real Faith*, Oxford: Monarch, 2009.

3. Flew, A., *There Is a God*, New York: HarperCollins, 2007, pp. 99ff.

Chapter 9

1. In *Christianity – A History*, Episode 7: 'God and the Scientists', Channel 4, Sunday 22 February 2009.

2. Darwin, F. (ed.), *The Autobiography of Charles Darwin and Selected Letters*, New York: Dover, 1958, p. 63.

3. Darwin wrote, in a letter to Asa Gray, though remaining agnostic. Cited in Brooke, J. H., 'The Relations Between Darwin's Science and his Religion' in Durant, J. (ed.), *Darwinism and Divinity*, Oxford: Blackwell, 1985, p. 56.

4. Bartholomew, D. J., *God, Chance and Purpose: Can God Have It Both Ways?*, Cambridge: Cambridge University Press, 2008, pp. 170–72.

5. An early TV programme, *The Blind Watchmaker*, BBC 2, *Horizon*, 19 January 1987.

6. Poole, M. W., 'A Critique of Aspects of the Philosophy and Theology of Richard Dawkins', *Science and Christian Belief*, Vol. 6 (1) (1994), p. 52.

7. Darwin, F. (ed.), *The Autobiography of Charles Darwin and*

Selected Letters, p. 249.

8. Christmas lecture 2.

9. Lewis, C. S., *The Problem of Pain*, London: Collins, 1957, p. 16.

10. Flew, A., *There Is a God*, p. 213.

11. Darwin, C., *The Origin of Species* (sixth [last] edition), London: John Murray, 1906, p. 658. (The citation first appeared in the second edition of 1860.)

12. Temple, W. F., *The Relations Between Religion and Science*, The Bampton Lectures for 1884, London: Macmillan, 1885, pp. 114f.

13. One of the phrases of Howard Van Till, Professor Emeritus of Physics and Astronomy, Calvin College, Grand Rapids, Michigan.

14. Dawkins, R., *River out of Eden*, London: Weidenfeld & Nicolson, 1995, pp. 76–83.

15. Dawkins, R., *The Blind Watchmaker*, London: Penguin, 1988, p. 6.

Chapter 10

1. Multiverse is the name given to hypothetical, multiple possible universes, of which ours is one.

2. Hawking, S. W., *Black Holes and Baby Universes and Other Essays*, London: Bantam Press, 1993, p. 150.

Index